HOT DOGS: THE LONG STORY

THE DISH ON THE DISH: A HISTORY OF YOUR FAVORITE FOODS

JULIE KNUTSON

CHERRY LAKE PRESS

Published in the United States of America by Cherry Lake Publishing Group
Ann Arbor, Michigan
www.cherrylakepublishing.com

Reading Adviser: Reading Adviser: Beth Walker Gambro, MS, Ed., Reading Consultant, Yorkville, IL
Photo Credits: © kcline/iStock.com, cover, 1; © Arina P Habich/Shutterstock.com, 5; © vitals/
    Shutterstock.com, 6; © a katz/Shutterstock.com, 9; © Courtesy of the Library of Congress, LC-DIG-
    ds-05428, 10; © carbonero/iStock.com, 12; © Stuart Monk/Shutterstock.com, 15; © Subbotina
    Anna/Shutterstock.com, 16; © John_P_Anderson/Shutterstock.com, 18; © Brent Hofacker/
    Shutterstock.com, 21; © Suzanne Pratt/Shutterstock.com, 23; © Arina P Habich/Shutterstock.com, 24;
    © JeniFoto/Shutterstock.com, 27; © Joshua Resnick/Shutterstock.com, 28

Library of Congress Cataloging-in-Publication Data

Names: Knutson, Julie, author.
Title: Hot dogs : the long story / Julie Knutson.
Description: Ann Arbor, Michigan : Cherry Lake Publishing, [2022] | Series: The dish on the dish : a history
    of your favorite foods | Includes bibliographical references and index. | Audience: Grades 4-6
Identifiers: LCCN 2021006191 (print) | LCCN 2021006192 (ebook) | ISBN 9781534187306 (hardcover) |
    ISBN 9781534188709 (paperback) | ISBN 9781534190108 (pdf) | ISBN 9781534191501 (ebook)
Subjects: LCSH: Cooking (Frankfurters)—Juvenile literature. | LCGFT: Cookbooks.
Classification: LCC TX749 .K58 2021 (print) | LCC TX749 (ebook) | DDC 641.6/6—dc23
LC record available at https://lccn.loc.gov/2021006191
LC ebook record available at https://lccn.loc.gov/2021006192

Cherry Lake Publishing Group would like to acknowledge the work of the Partnership for 21st Century
Learning, a Network of Battelle for Kids. Please visit http://www.battelleforkids.org/networks/p21
for more information.

Printed in the United States of America
Corporate Graphics

ABOUT THE AUTHOR

Julie Knutson is an author who lives in northern Illinois with her husband, son, and border
collie. She prefers her pancakes with Nutella and bananas, her pizza "Detroit-style," and her
mac 'n' cheese with little green peas.

TABLE OF CONTENTS

First Plating

This handheld food has delighted generations of baseball fans and backyard barbecuers. When Mickey Mouse made his first movie in 1929, its name was the first thing he said. It's been spawned into the shape of a giant car, inspired a LEGO® minifigure, and sparked a long rivalry between New York and Chicago, Illinois. It can be boiled, grilled, fried, or roasted on a stick. It goes by many names, including franks, frankfurters, wieners, and red hots.

It is a truly **iconic** American food. It is . . . the HOT DOG!

Today, Americans eat an estimated 20 billion hot dogs a year. That amounts to roughly 60 hot dogs per person. Around the world, you can find unique regional versions of it. But where and when did it start? And how did this totally tubular food get to be one of the most recognized in the world?

Popular hot dog condiments include ketchup, mustard, and relish.

First, a simple question: Just what is a hot dog? At its most basic, a hot dog is an **oblong**, precooked sausage served in a bun. Hot dogs can be made of finely minced beef, pork, poultry, or a combination of those meats. In recent years, veggie dogs have even hit the market to satisfy those who crave a plant-based version.

Hot dogs are the culinary grandchildren of European sausages. During the 18th and 19th centuries, food traditions traveled with immigrants as they moved to new places. People from many countries

enjoyed the ancestors of today's hot dogs. In Germany and Austria, people ate them during winter as a **cured** food. As hot dog historian Bruce Kraig notes, sausages were also sold at markets and fairs throughout Europe from the Middle Ages onward.

In both central Europe and the United States, sausages were often served with bread. But the pairing of a sausage with a custom-size, sliced bun is the product of a specific time and place. In 1867, German immigrant Charles Feltman was working as a baker in Brooklyn, New York. Around this time, New Yorkers started flocking to the seaside neighborhood of Coney Island during summers. Feltman spent a few years selling his baked goods on the beach but soon realized that his customers wanted something they could eat for lunch. This lunch needed to be easy to eat while strolling or enjoying popular amusements, without needing silverware.

Feltman's roommate worked at a meat processing plant, and they paired up to create a lunch treat. Feltman used his baking skills to create a long bun. Soon, he was selling this bun—stuffed with a sausage and topped with mustard, sauerkraut, and chopped onions—from a converted pie cart. In his first summer of business, he sold 3,684 of the items he called "red hots" at 5 cents each.

While pork sausages were popular early in U.S. history, that changed as immigrants arrived from different parts of the world. In the mid-19th century, Jewish sausage makers in New York and Chicago, Illinois, replaced pork, which isn't **kosher***, with beef. As Americans became increasingly concerned about the quality of their meat, kosher was branded as cleaner and safer. All-beef hot dogs became favorites in Jewish and non-Jewish communities alike.*

Business was so good that within a few years, he opened a restaurant, Feltman's Ocean Pavilion. Eventually, his business served not only food at its nine restaurants, but also offered a hotel, gardens, a carousel, a roller coaster, an outdoor movie theater, and an **Alpine** village! In its heyday, it was the largest restaurant in the world, cranking out 40,000 red hots daily.

Success never goes unnoticed. By the 1910s, other red hot **vendors** sprung up to compete with Feltman's. The biggest rival? Nathan's®, still a fixture of Coney Island's boardwalk today. Nathan's® was born in one of the kitchens of Feltman's Ocean Pavilion, where Polish immigrant Nathan Handwerker spent weekends slicing bread for red hots. Legend says that Handwerker was so poor that he slept on the kitchen's floor and survived on a diet of Feltman's sausage.

Nathan's® Hot Dog Eating Contest is held on the Fourth of July. It has been held annually at Coney Island since the 1970s.

A change of fortune came for Handwerker when he got a loan from two former Feltman's employees who hit it big in the entertainment business. They were famous singers Jimmy Durante and Eddie Cantor. The pair lent Nathan $300 to set up his own stand, from which he would sell red hots for 5 cents each. Feltman had increased its prices to 10 cents, so Handwerker's dog was a bargain. Nathan's® was a success and continued to grow through the years. Today, Nathan's® is more than a restaurant. Its products are sold in more than 55,000 stores in 10 countries.

A 1947 photo showing crowds lined up to receive Nathan's® hot dogs.

Elsewhere in the United States, red hots were introduced to new audiences through events like the Chicago World's Fair of 1893 in Illinois. At this event attended by 27 million people, meat **entrepreneur** Oscar Mayer sold his sausages alongside dozens of other vendors. The food got another boost at a 1901 New York Giants baseball game. On an unusually cold day, a quick-thinking caterer swapped ice cream for hot sausage sandwiches. They were an immediate fan favorite. Through newspaper articles, popular songs, and advertisements, red hots were soon a well-known food. People associated them with carefree pleasures like the beach and ballpark.

That's not to say that people didn't have their concerns about what went into their hot dogs. In the late 1800s and early 1900s, sausages were frequently made from scrap animal organs and muscle. Fillers and extenders were also often added to the mix. Conditions in meat processing plants were far from **sanitary**.

Coney Island

As the United States became **industrialized** in the 19th century, people had more leisure time. New amusement centers with food, games, and rides like carousels offered people a place to spend their spare time and money. In New York, Coney Island was one such place.

Located in southwest Brooklyn, the seaside neighborhood attracted city dwellers looking to escape the summer heat. By 1873, it drew 25,000 to 30,000 visitors each weekend. At its peak between the 1880s and 1940s, it was the largest amusement complex in the United States. People there enjoyed roller coasters, boardwalks, bath houses, and racetracks. There was something for everyone, and people of different social classes mingled in this new social space. Still, it wasn't fully democratic. Discriminatory practices seen elsewhere in the United States were there in the form of **segregated** bath houses and beaches.

Dachshunds are also called "wiener dogs" because of their long, narrow build.

Books like Upton Sinclair's 1906 novel *The Jungle* spotlighted their unclean operations. For some, it wasn't a stretch to think that the meat of other animals—including dogs—might make its way into the final product.

The oblong shape also reminded people of a dog breed, the dachshund. One story says that cartoonist T. A. Dorgan captured the crowd's reception of the new food at that cold 1901 Giants game. According to legend, Dorgan thought the sandwich looked like the long-and-low German dog but didn't want to risk spelling "dachshund." Instead, he used the much simpler "hot dog." While this is a great story, the name "hot dog" was actually used in the 1890s. Food historians trace the first printed use of "hot dog" to a Yale University humor magazine early in that decade. From there, it spread to other colleges and beyond. In the new century, the hot dog would become a mass-produced food of the future.

CHAPTER 2

Migrations

In the early 20th century, hot dog stands and carts sprung up in cities from Detroit, Michigan, to Los Angeles, California. Like the hamburger, another handheld food that gained fame in the same era, hot dogs offered a quick, convenient meal for working people. In Detroit, two legendary restaurants started serving "Coneys" slathered in chili, mustard, and onions to hungry autoworkers. This distinctive regional style was developed by Greek and Macedonian immigrants who named it after the birthplace of the red hot.

There are 3,100 hot dog stand licenses in New York City, New York.

As technologies changed, so did the hot dog. For generations, making sausage was a time-consuming process. Meat products had to be ground, hand-stuffed into casings, linked, and cured. In the late 1800s, steam-driven meat choppers and stuffers came into use. Those were followed by electric machines that made the process even speedier. After the publication of books like *The Jungle*, machine-processed meats held some appeal. To many people, industrial food represented food free from human **contamination**.

On the Fourth of July, Americans consume 150 million hot dogs.

In the 1920s and 1930s, companies like Oscar Mayer®, Sabrett®, and Nathan's® built their brands. In 1929, Oscar Mayer® started wrapping their hot dogs in a yellow band. This allowed consumers to quickly recognize a brand associated with high quality. In the 1930s, Sabrett® gave free umbrellas to all street cart vendors in New York City, New York. Even today, umbrellas with the Sabrett® logo are seen on many hot dog carts in the city. Nathan's® was so successful that President Franklin D. Roosevelt served their hot dogs to the king and queen of the United Kingdom in 1939. The next day, the *New York Times* headline screamed, "KING TRIES HOT DOGS AND ASKS FOR MORE."

However, it wasn't until 1972 that a formal competition was established. Today, the event is broadcast on ESPN. More than 35,000 people watch the contest on-site. The record, held by Joey Chestnut, is 75 hot dogs in 10 minutes.

After World War II, engineers at Oscar Mayer® and other major meat producers worked to streamline production through **continuous flow processing**. Oscar Mayer® developed a system

A Fourth of July Tradition

Every year on the Fourth of July, crowds gather on Coney Island's boardwalk. They're not just there to splash in the waves or scream on roller coasters. Many are there to watch Nathan's® Annual Hot Dog Eating Contest.

Legend says that the first hot dog eating contest happened on July 4, 1916. Nathan Handwerker was working at his stand when he overheard a group of immigrant men arguing about who was the "most American." Handwerker said that there was an easy way to settle the argument. Whomever could eat the most hot dogs in 12 minutes would take the title. The contest was won by James Mullen from Ireland, who downed 13 hot dogs in that time.

There are currently six different Wienermobiles traveling around the United States.

that employees dubbed the "Wiener Tunnel" and the "Hot Dog Highway." In an hour from start to finish, meats were shuttled along a 10-lane "superhighway." They were wrapped in plastic at the end, ready for shipment to supermarkets. While Oscar Mayer® processed about 10,000 hot dogs in one hour, another operation in Des Moines, Iowa, was producing 56,000 dogs every hour.

This surge in production met the needs of young families, who needed quick, convenient foods. After World War II, a period called the **baby boom** led to a great increase in population. During the 1950s and 1960s, the American economy was prospering. The expansion of highways also made the **suburbs** more appealing to Americans who could afford to move. Companies started to target ads specifically to kids. Oscar Mayer® had a fleet of "Wienermobiles," vehicles shaped like giant hot dogs. Children who flocked to this imaginative set of wheels were greeted by "Little Oscar," a chef who handed out whistles. Through these types of promotions, hot dogs became a food people ate throughout their whole lives. This food wasn't just linked to places like the ballpark or the beach. It was also linked to the idea of being a kid.

The Oscar Mayer® Wienermobile still cruises interstate highways today! The first of these vehicles hit the road in 1936. According to food historian Bruce Kraig, the idea came out of "the company's wiener wagon that traveled around Chicago, Illinois, with a German band serenading sausage lovers."

CHAPTER 3

Evolution and Wild Variations

Like pizza, hamburgers, tacos, and many other foods, hot dogs provide a base on which people and cultures express themselves. The types of hot dogs you eat and the way you make them say a lot about how and where you live in the world. Let's take a look at different takes on this food item around the globe.

A New York-style hot dog is usually simply prepared. The sausage is grilled and topped with mustard, onions, and sauerkraut. In contrast, the Chicago-style hot dog is often called "a garden in a bun." That's because Chicago-style dogs blended their sellers'

Chili, cheese, and onions make hearty toppings for hot dogs.

Central and Eastern European roots with the vegetables offered by Mediterranean vendors. In addition to mustard and onions, these dogs are topped with tomatoes, pickles, hot peppers, and bright green relish.

Travel south and west from Chicago, Illinois, to Hermosillo, Mexico, home of the Sonoran dog. The sausage itself is wrapped in a robe of bacon. Then, it's stuffed into a roll and topped with avocado, refried beans, cheese, onions, tomatoes, jalapeño salsa, mayo, and mustard.

Head to Colombia for another unique treat. Sure, there's ketchup, mustard, and mayo. But there's also crushed potato chips. And pineapple. And sometimes even three quail eggs. You definitely won't be hungry after this meal!

State fairs are the sites where wacky and experimental foods happen. At the 2019 Kansas State Fair, vendors offered new variations on the traditional dog, They included a hot dog stuffed in a jelly doughnut and topped with bacon, plus a corn dog dipped in chocolate, with sprinkles. What do you think? Would you try these wild concoctions?

The Sonoran dog combines the flavors of Mexico and the United States.

Hot dogs have been enjoyed at the park, at home, and even in space!

Next up? Iceland, where you'll request not a hot dog, but a pylsur. It's not just a combo of pork and beef in this dog. Lamb gets added to the mix. Typically, it's topped with an apple-infused ketchup, a mayo sauce, and fried and fresh onions.

Can't decide between a hot dog and pizza? In Amsterdam, the Netherlands, you can get a hybrid. Here, it's not uncommon for stands to serve up a sausage roll topped with pizza sauce and mozzarella cheese. Those ingredients are then all put under a broiler to melt together.

Lastly, travel to Japan. Here, your hot dog gets transformed into something else entirely—an octopus! That's right, in kid-friendly **bento boxes**, sausages frequently get sliced up to look like an eight-legged sea creature. To make them extra tasty, they're fried.

CHAPTER 4

Make Your Own!

In Kansas City, Kansas, it's a sesame bun, sauerkraut, and melted Swiss cheese. In the Philippines, it's a notched hot dog with a side of rice, an egg, and banana ketchup. And in Idaho? It's served in a baked potato, of course! But have you ever heard of a carrot hot dog? Give it a try!

INGREDIENTS:

- 8 peeled carrots, cut to hot dog length
- 8 hot dog buns
- 1 cup (250 milliliters) soy sauce
- 2 tablespoons (30 ml) liquid smoke
- 2 tablespoons (30 ml) Worcestershire sauce
- 2 tablespoons (30 ml) maple syrup
- 2 tablespoons (30 ml) ketchup
- 2 cups (500 ml) water

Vegan carrot hot dogs can be topped with all sorts of colorful vegetables.

DIRECTIONS:

1. In a medium saucepan, whisk together soy sauce, liquid smoke, Worcestershire sauce, maple syrup, ketchup, and water.

2. Add the peeled and trimmed carrots. Bring to a boil.

3. Reduce heat to medium, and let carrots simmer for 8 to 10 minutes.

4. Remove the pan from the heat and let sit for 15 to 20 minutes.

5. Remove carrots from the liquid and serve on buns with desired toppings.

Congratulations on trying something new!

Corn dogs are hot dogs fried in cornmeal batter.
Having a stick makes them easier to eat.

Grilling Up 10 Fascinating Facts About Hot Dogs

- In the United States, National Hot Dog Day is celebrated each July 22.

- Joey Chestnut holds the world record for the most hot dogs eaten in 10 minutes. Chestnut ate 75 hot dogs during the 2020 Nathan's® contest to score the record and his 13th championship title.

- On the Fourth of July, if all the hot dogs Americans ate were stretched in a line, it could link Washington, D.C., and Los Angeles, California, more than five times!

- Think New Yorkers or Chicagoans eat the most hot dogs in the United States? Think again! The title goes to people in Los Angeles, California.

- *Apollo 11* astronauts Neil Armstrong and Buzz Aldrin ate hot dogs on their trip to the Moon in 1969. The hot dogs were one of the first foods eaten on the Moon.

- The world's longest hot dog measured more than 668 feet (204 meters)! It was made in Paraguay in 2011.

- In Wisconsin, Milwaukee Brewers fans cheer on their favorite sausage in a race at the bottom of the sixth inning of each home game. They choose from bratwurst, Polish sausage, Italian sausage, hot dog, and chorizo.

- In 2013, black hot dogs dyed with edible bamboo charcoal were a food trend in Tokyo, Japan.

- Scientists estimate that 83 is the human limit for hot dog consumption in 10 minutes.

- How much did the world's most expensive hot dog cost? In 2014, a hot dog topped with caviar, maitake mushrooms, and shaved truffles fetched $169 at Seattle's Tokyo Dog Food Truck in Washington.

Timeline

1871   Charles Feltman makes the move from red hot vendor to restaurant owner.

1894   A Yale University humor magazine labels a sausage delivery cart a "dog wagon."

1906   The publication of Upton Sinclair's *The Jungle* leads to new federal regulations of food safety. Oscar Mayer® is one of the first companies to pledge to comply with the inspections.

1916   Nathan Handwerker opens Nathan's®, selling 5-cent hot dogs to Coney Island beachgoers.

1929   Mickey Mouse speaks his first words on film with the exclamation, "Hot dog!"

1936   The Oscar Mayer® Wienermobile begins driving around the United States.

1939   President Franklin D. Roosevelt and his wife, Eleanor, serve hot dogs to the king and queen of the United Kingdom at a garden party.

1969   Buzz Aldrin and Neal Armstrong take hot dogs to the Moon.

1972   The first official Nathan's® Hot Dog Eating Contest takes place on July 4.

2020   Joey Chestnut sets a new world record by eating 75 hot dogs in 10 minutes at Nathan's® Hot Dog Eating Contest.